LIVING JEWISH VALUES

VOLUME 3

T0198372

Be a Good Friend

Aviva Werner

BEHRMAN HOUSE

Behrman House, Inc.

www.behrmanhouse.com

In memory of my beloved mother, Frieda Zablow a"h,
who spelled her name Frieda as in friend.

Aviva Werner

Design: **Jill A. Winitzer, WinitzerDesign.com**

The publisher gratefully acknowledges the following sources of photographs and graphic images:
(T=top, B=bottom)

Cover Pressmaster/Shutterstock; ii Monkey Business Images/Shutterstock; 2 Iv Mirin/Shutterstock; 3 Atlaspix/Shutterstock; 4 Kittisak/Shutterstock; 6, 36 Canicula/Shutterstock; 7 Arkady Mazor/Shutterstock; 8T Darko Zeljkovic/Shutterstock; 8B Andrey Shadrin/Shutterstock; 9T Maridav/Shutterstock; 9B Vincent St. Thomas/Shutterstock; 11, 21, 31, 41 Lena Sergeeva/Shutterstock; 12 auremar/Shutterstock; 14 RAGMA IMAGES/Shutterstock; 16T PT Images/Shutterstock; 16B Lisa S. /Shutterstock; 17T AISPIX by Image Source/Shutterstock; 17B Olga Dmitrieva/Shutterstock; 18 Antonio Abrignani/Shutterstock; 19 Angela Buxton; 22 courtyardpix/Shutterstock; 23 Yayayoyo/Shutterstock; 24 Marish/Shutterstock; 26 Hein Nouwens/Shutterstock; 27 Stephen Voss; 28T joyfuldesigns/Shutterstock; 28B dotshock/Shutterstock; 29T kroomjai/Shutterstock; 29B Jaimie Duplass/Shutterstock; 30 cromic/Shutterstock; 32 Nicku/Shutterstock; 33 DOUG RAPHAEL/Shutterstock; 37 Alan Sussman; 38T Lisa F. Young/Shutterstock; 38B bepsy/Shutterstock; 39T Dani Vincek/Shutterstock; 39B MANDY GODBEHEAR/Shutterstock; 40 Gesha/Shutterstock; 43 Casablanka/ Shutterstock

Copyright ©2013 Behrman House, Inc.
Springfield, New Jersey
ISBN 978-0-87441-872-9
Manufactured in the United States of America

Library of Congress Cataloging-in-Publication Data
Werner, Aviva.
Be a good friend / Aviva Werner.
    page. cm -- (Living Jewish values ; volume 3)
ISBN 978-0-87441-872-9
1. Jewish religious education--Textbooks for children. 2. Friendship--Religious aspects--Judaism--Textbooks. 3. Jewish ethics--Textbooks. 4. Jewish way of life--Textbooks. I. Title.
BM105.W46 2013
296.3'6--dc23
                        2012043327

CONTENTS

INTRODUCTION

The insistent knocking brought Hillel to his feet. He opened the door to find a man on his doorstep, a look of belligerence in his eyes. "Teach me the entire Torah while I stand on one foot," the visitor challenged him. But Hillel the sage was up to the challenge. "What is hateful to you, don't do to your friend," he replied. "That is the whole Torah; the rest is commentary; go and learn it." (Shabbat 31a)

According to Hillel's statement, Judaism's core teachings relate to how we treat our friends. In fact, the Torah explicitly instructs us to treasure our friends—"Love your neighbor as yourself" (Leviticus 19:18)—and to consider their needs to be as serious to us as our own. We are taught to return a lost object, to feed the poor, and to tell the truth, for example, because doing so will help us build relationships of honesty, integrity, trust, compassion, and respect.

RT @Taanit **"I have learned a lot from my teachers, and even more from my friends."** #Talmud

This book, *Be a Good Friend*, is volume 3 in the *Living Jewish Values* series. In it, you will explore four Jewish values that are important in forming and strengthening friendships:

Dan L'chaf Zechut—Judging Favorably

Reyut—Friendship

Koach Hadibur—The Power of Speech

Ometz Lev—Courage

The legends and role model profiles you will read in each chapter provide concrete examples of the Torah's view of friendship, the personality quizzes and journal activities encourage you to evaluate your own friendships, and the strategy activities give you practical tips on how to bring these Jewish values into your life. When you build your personal friendships on Jewish values, you form a bond that is deeply meaningful and satisfying, and you grow as a person in the process. Now, to borrow from the words of Hillel, "Go and learn it!"

CHAPTER 1

Dan L'chaf Zechut

Peninah, who had seven children, never missed an opportunity to taunt the childless Hannah and remind her of her infertility. The teasing hurt Hannah deeply. One day, when Hannah felt particularly sad, she turned her anguish into prayer. It was a silent prayer in the Holy Temple. She moved her lips as she poured out her heart, but her voice could not be heard. Eli, the high priest, saw Hannah but mistook her silent supplication for drunkenness. He scolded her, "How long will you be a drunkard? Sober up!" "No," she corrected him, "I am a woman in pain. I didn't drink any alcohol. I only poured out my soul before God." *(I Samuel 1)*

Judging Favorably

Eli the priest made a huge mistake. When confronted with an unfamiliar face in a new situation, he jumped to conclusions. Unfortunately, things like this happen all the time when we let biased first impressions hijack our understanding. When we jump to conclusions or allow prejudice to cloud our judgment, we risk acting inappropriately or hurting other people, as Eli the priest did.

Being דָּן לְכַף זְכוּת (*dan l'chaf zechut*) means giving people the benefit of the doubt, even if their behavior appears negative at first blush. We shouldn't rush to attack, judge, or get angry at someone else's behavior. Rather, we must approach these unknowns with a positive outlook and search for merit.

JUDGING FRIENDS

. . . .

Giving the benefit of the doubt isn't limited to first impressions. When your best friend says she can't hang out because she's grounded, what do you think when you catch her at the mall? When you've texted your friend a bunch of times and he's not texting you back, what do you conclude? When you overhear your friend spilling your secrets, how do you react?

Maimonides, the medieval Jewish philosopher and Torah scholar, teaches, "When someone who is known to be righteous and has a reputation for good deeds is seen doing an action that seems to be bad, and the only way of considering it good is through really stretching things and assuming a very remote possibility, it is still obligatory to interpret it as good based on that possibility." Your friend's past history and reputation should inform how you judge her now. Maybe there's more to the story than just what you saw or heard.

ACTIVITY 1

Dan l'chaf zechut *literally means "judge on a scale of merit." Before digital bathroom scales, people weighed things on scales like the one below. This scale is tipped to the side of merit. Which statements listed here reflect favorable judgment and which reflect jumping to conclusions? Draw a line to the appropriate side of the scale.*

merit

fault

Maybe I misunderstood.

I'm sure it's his fault.

There has got to be more to the story.

That's very suspicious.

Give her a break.

His heart is in the right place.

He is being rude and inconsiderate.

How dare she behave that way?

I'm sure I don't see the whole picture here.

What a terrible thing to do!

How Good a Batter Are You?

Take this quiz and find out.

The party starts in ten minutes, but your ride is late. When your friend and her mother finally show up, you:

◆ Smile because you assume that they would have been on time if possible.

◆ Spend the whole ride worrying that you're missing some of the fun.

◆ Look at your watch and then go to the car with a scowl on your face.

You haven't met the new kid, but she's just been placed in your group for a big project. You:

◆ Look forward to hearing her fresh, new perspective on the work you've done.

◆ Make sure that she contributes to the project in a way that won't affect your grade.

◆ Worry that your group will lose valuable time explaining everything to her.

Toward the end of the fifth inning, your teammate misses an easy catch. You:

◆ Wonder if something's bothering him or if he's having some kind of trouble.

◆ Realize that you'll have to play more aggressively to help the team.

◆ Grunt angrily because you think he shouldn't have made the team.

Your friend said he was coming to see you perform in the school play, but he didn't show up. You:

◆ Tell him that you missed him and accept his explanation as the truth.

◆ Hope that he'll hear about how well you performed.

◆ Figure that he probably wasn't interested.

Mostly red
Home run

When faced with a difficult situation, you are happy to give people the benefit of the doubt. By judging others favorably, you are following the commandment to "judge others in righteousness" *(Leviticus 19:15).*

Mostly green
Foul

Like the player who makes a foul, you've lost an opportunity for the moment. Since you don't know another person's intentions, you are happy to think about your own needs rather than judge anyone else. You are trying to follow the advice of Hillel, who said, "Do not judge people until you've been in their place" *(Pirkei Avot 2:5).*

Mostly blue
Strike

You may be trying to judge people objectively, but you are probably missing the ball a lot of the time. Why not take a more positive approach? You could try to follow this advice from Rashi: "Unless one knows otherwise for sure, one should assume that other people's actions are all good" *(Rashi on Pirkei Avot 1:6).*

AGADDIC TRADITION

Before he was a great Torah scholar, Rabbi Akiva was a simple laborer. A wealthy landowner once hired him for a three-year job in southern Israel. When the work was finished, Akiva asked his well-to-do boss for his payment.

"I don't have any money," the boss said curtly.

"You can pay me with animals," suggested Akiva. After all, he thought, "I can sell them in the market and recover my wages that way."

But Akiva's boss answered, "I don't have any animals."

Akiva offered to accept other forms of payment, including land and even bed linens. But the boss insisted that he had nothing. Dejected, Akiva returned home after three years with nothing to show for his hard work.

Two weeks later, Akiva's boss showed up at his door and handed Akiva the payment. "When you asked me for your money," he said, "and I denied having any, what did you think of me?"

"I thought you probably had come across a great sale and used up all your money buying merchandise for your business," answered Akiva.

"And when you asked me for animals and I said I didn't have any, what did you think then?"

"I thought you probably had rented your sheep and cattle to others. I thought you probably rented out your land, too, which is why you denied having any. And when I asked for the other things, like pillows and blankets, I thought you might have donated them to the Holy Temple."

As it turns out, Akiva was right on all accounts. In addition to paying up his wages, the boss offered the hard-working Akiva a blessing: "Just as you judged me favorably, so may God judge you favorably."

ACTIVITY 2

Akiva judged his boss favorably by thinking up possible scenarios to explain his boss's odd behavior. What other possible scenarios can you think of? _____

_____

How could the boss have made it easier for Akiva to give him the benefit of the doubt? _____

_____

_____

Dan L'Chaf Zechut Superstar: Rabbi Aryeh Levin

Rabbi Aryeh Levin was known in Jerusalem as a friend to every Jew. He visited Jewish inmates in the prison and Jewish patients in the leper hospital. His tireless efforts on behalf of the poor, sick, and heartbroken earned him the nickname "*tzaddik* [righteous person] of Jerusalem." Rabbi Levin was particularly well known for judging everyone favorably, a behavior he attributed to a funeral and a flower pot.

One day, Rabbi Aryeh Levin attended the funeral of Rabbi Eliezer Rivlin, a well-respected community leader. As the funeral procession wound its way through the streets of Jerusalem in the direction of the cemetery, Rabbi Levin spied someone leaving the procession. The man, who Rabbi Levin recognized as the late Rabbi Rivlin's best friend, ducked into a flower shop and bought a flower pot. Deeply disturbed, Rabbi Levin wondered aloud, "Is this how a man acts toward a true friend who has passed away—a friend who treated him so well while he was alive? Couldn't he find some other time to buy a flower pot?"

Unable to contain his feelings, Rabbi Levin approached the man and rebuked him to his face. "Rabbi Rivlin was your closest friend for thirty years! How could you leave his funeral procession to go shopping?"

"Please let me explain," said the man, flower pot in hand. "For years I have been visiting a patient with leprosy. He died yesterday, and the doctors ordered that all his clothes and belongings, even his tefillin, be burned because leprosy is contagious. I begged the doctors to let me bury the holy tefillin in accordance with our religious law instead of burning them. The doctor would only agree if I would bring a clay pot today before noon. The tefillin would be placed in the pot and then buried in the ground. So you see, I had to leave Rabbi Rivlin's funeral so I could get the clay pot in time. I had no choice."

"Since then," said Rabbi Levin, "I firmly resolved to judge every person favorably."

Dan L'chaf Zechut

Here are four situations that call for being *dan l'chaf zechut.* Help strengthen these friendships by thinking of possible scenarios to explain each not-so-nice behavior.

"Why isn't she returning my calls? She must be ignoring me!"

She can't return your calls because _____
_____
_____.

She tried calling, but can't get through because
_____
_____.

She did return your call, but you don't know about it because _____
_____
_____.

"We made plans to hang out. He stood me up and is making me look like a fool! "

He can't come because _____
_____
_____.

He came, but couldn't find you because _____
_____
_____.

He wanted to come, but wasn't able to because _____
_____
_____.

Photo Gallery

"I saw her last night and she wasn't studying. She must have cheated!"

She knew this material well even without studying because _____ _____ _____ _____.

She did study, but you don't know that because _____ _____ _____ _____.

"My notebook was on this desk. Who took it?"

You're looking in the wrong place because _____ _____ _____.

Your notebook had to be moved because _____ _____ _____

ACTIVITY 3 ....

In addition to the obligation to give others the benefit of the doubt, Jews also have an obligation to avoid giving others the wrong impression of our own actions, called marit ayin. *Follow the example provided and fill in each empty box with the appropriate information.*

	HOW IT MAY APPEAR TO MY FRIEND	THE TRUTH	PREVENTIVE STRATEGY
My friend asks if he can borrow the earbuds from my iPod for a minute. I say no (because I have misplaced them). A half hour later, I find them in the back of my locker, so I use them during recess.	I lied.	I only said no because I couldn't find my earbuds at the time.	As soon as I find them, I could tell my friend and offer to lend them to him now if he still needs them.
I proudly announce to my friend that I got an A on the math test. A second after I say it, I remember how this friend has been struggling in math lately. I want to bite my tongue.			
My best friend and I went to different overnight camps. We promised to e-mail each other every day, but it turned out that my camp had a "no technology" rule. When I came home, my friend gave me the cold shoulder.			
My family is moving to a new house, but I haven't told anyone yet. One day my friend Lily is talking to another friend, Sasha, whose mother happens to be my parents' real estate agent. "So, when are they moving?" Sasha asks Lily. Lily tries to be vague, not wanting to let Sasha know that it's news to her.			

WHAT I THINK

Giving people the benefit of the doubt and seeing the positive in their actions is the foundation of positive, constructive relationships.

1. Describe a time when you made an assumption about someone's actions, only to be proved wrong. How could you have prevented this?

2. Describe a time when someone made mistaken assumptions about your actions. What could you have done to prevent the other person from making these mistaken assumptions?

3. Describe a time when you had the feeling that another person would understand you better if he or she were in your place or situation.

4. How have these experiences affected how you judge others?

5. Choose a story you have heard or read recently that has a mean or "bad" character. Retell the story from that character's perspective, trying to judge his or her actions favorably. How easy or hard is it to change your mind about someone?

CHAPTER 2

Reyut

Job was on top of the world. He had a nice family, plenty of money, and a happy home. Then came a decree that ruined everything. All of his possessions were stolen, burned, or destroyed; his children died when their house was hit by a freak windstorm; and Job himself came down with a nasty case of boils. When Job's three friends heard about the tragedies, they traveled seven hundred miles to mourn with him. The Book of Job tells us that they sat with him on the ground for seven days, but no one said a word, for they saw that he was in great pain. *(Job)*

Friendship

Real friends stick together when times get tough. If one falls, the other lends support. If one needs to talk, the other listens. And if one needs silence, as Job did, a friend sits quietly. The Jewish value of רֵעוּת *(reyut)* requires a foundation of sharing, trust, and respect.

Because being a friend means sharing experiences, expressing empathy, and learning from others, the bond of friendship strengthens one's personality and enables a person to grow. By nurturing each other, good friends can cultivate spiritual, emotional, and intellectual growth in one another.

POPULARITY

We tend to measure our worth by how many people invite us to parties, text us, and like us on Facebook. We think that hundreds of Facebook connections translates to hundreds of friends and, as a result, happiness. But it doesn't. According to a 2012 study by researchers at Western Illinois University, having hundreds of Facebook friends leads not to happiness, but to shallow friendships and an exaggerated self-image.

We don't need hundreds or even tens of friends to be happy, only that one true friend with whom to share our deepest, truest selves. True friendship means more than just a click of the mouse or an invitation to a bowling party. It means sharing, caring, and investment.

ACTIVITY 1

When choosing friends, we must remember to focus on the character of others, not on what we can get from them. Write a want ad seeking a friend.

What qualities should a friend possess? How much is a friend worth?

Why is it important to select a friend carefully? _____

_____

_____

What type of person would make a poor friend? _____

_____

_____

What Do You Look for in a Friend?

Take this quiz and find out.

In the store, you thought these bright orange sneakers were pretty cool. But now that you've bought them, you wonder if they're tacky. Your best friend should:

◆ Assure you they are cool and that you are a definite trendsetter.

◆ Suggest you try them out for a few weeks around the neighborhood and see how you feel.

◆ Spare you the social humiliation and tell you straight-up that the sneakers look ridiculous.

You're thinking of trying out for the basketball team, even though your jump shot and dribbling could use a lot of work. A good friend should:

◆ Remind you how great you are on defense and that a good coach values a positive attitude.

◆ Suggest that you join an intramural league this year and go for Junior Varsity next season.

◆ Tell you not to get your hopes up because chances are pretty slim you'll make the cut.

Your brownies for the bake sale turn out more black than brown. When your friend does a taste test, you hope he'll:

◆ Tell you that you're the next Betty Crocker, since he knows you're a bit sensitive.

◆ Assure you they're pretty good but suggest you put in another batch for a little less time.

◆ Suggest you throw this batch away since you don't want to feel embarrassed.

You've been working on a documentary for school and show it to a friend. The feedback you'd most value is:

◆ "Don't change a thing! This should be aired on the Sundance channel!"

◆ "Overall, it's really good, but the ending could use some more work."

◆ "The ending is very long. What if you tried something like this instead …?"

Mostly red
Sweet

As far as you're concerned, good friends should be nice and sweet, giving each other a boost of self-confidence. After all, as we read in the Talmud (*Shabbat 133b*), "Just as God is gracious and compassionate, you should also be gracious and compassionate."

Mostly green
Balanced

Just the right balance of praise and honest feedback is what you expect from your friends. As Maimonides teaches, it is best to walk the middle path, finding a comfortable medium between extremes (*Mishneh Torah, Hilchot Dei'ot 1: 4–7*).

Mostly blue
Truthful

The Talmud advises us to "love criticism, for as long as there is criticism in the world, pleasantness comes to the world, good and blessing come to the world" (*Tamid 28a*), and you've taken this to heart. You most appreciate a friend who will tell it to you straight, even when the truth is a bit hard to take.

Reyut

For some people, making a friend is as easy as introducing themselves with a friendly smile. For others, it's harder. These teens are struggling with making friends and keeping them. What advice can you offer to help them build positive relationships?

Challenge: *"I'm shy."*

Advice: _____
_____
_____

How might you introduce yourself to a new acquaintance? _____
_____
_____

What could you ask new acquaintances about themselves? _____
_____
_____

Challenge: *"We used to be good friends, but now we're in a fight."*

Advice: _____
_____
_____

How can you make the first move to restoring peace? ___
_____
_____

How can you reinforce the positive aspects of your relationship? _____
_____
_____

Photo Gallery

Challenge: *"It's impossible to break into their clique."*

Advice: _____
_____
_____

Why do people want to break into cliques? ____
_____
_____

What should you do if you and your friends have different ideas about what's fun to do together? _____
_____
_____

Challenge: *"I'm the new kid. In my old school I had tons of friends. Here I don't know anyone."*

Advice: _____
_____
_____

Where do you like to go to socialize? _____
_____
_____
_____

Where are good places to meet new people? List three. _____
_____
_____

friendship **17**

AGADDIC TRADITION

Choni made friends in the study hall, not on the playing field. One day, on his way there, Choni met an old man planting a tree.

"How long will it take for this tree to bear fruit?" he asked.

"About seventy years," answered the old man.

"Why plant a tree if you know you might not live to enjoy its fruit?" probed the young man.

The old man scratched the earth with his shovel before answering. "Just as my ancestors made sure that I would find fruit trees when I came into the world," he explained, "I am making sure that my descendants will have fruit trees when they come into the world."

Feeling exhausted, Choni lay down near the baby carob tree for a nap. The short rest turned into a deep slumber that lasted seventy years. When he woke up, Choni stared in disbelief at the grown tree, now filled with ripe fruit. "What's going on?" he wondered.

Searching for answers, Choni headed to the study hall to find his friends. Everything there, however, looked strange, including the faces that looked up at him when he entered.

"Your friends passed away years ago," the students told him when he asked about several people by name.

Feeling lonely and despondent, Choni reached out to the strangers the only way he knew how—through Torah study. As he explained a particularly difficult concept, a young man marveled, "I'm told that Choni would give clear explanations like that!"

"I am Choni," he revealed.

Peals of laughter rang throughout the study hall.

"Choni disappeared seventy years ago," someone shouted.

"I tell you, I'm Choni," he insisted, but no one believed him.

Crushed, Choni fled the study hall. "Either friendship or death," he cried out. And with that, his soul was gathered up and brought to heaven.

ACTIVITY 2

When is it good to be alone? When is it not good to be alone? _____

_____

What is it like to be lonely? _____

_____

How can you reach out in friendship to someone you know who may be lonely? _____

_____

REYUT SUPERSTAR: ANGELA BUXTON

The crowd's jeers and hoots quiet to a hush as the underdog, Althea Gibson, ties the score. The sudden silence is broken only by the tennis ball's rhythmic contact with the rackets of Angela Buxton and Althea Gibson. It is the semifinals of the French Championship in 1957.

Suddenly, several points into the third set, Althea strikes the ball with the full power of her forehand, and the strap of her tennis dress snaps. With eight thousand people watching her every move, Althea freezes in utter embarrassment, and the crowd erupts in wild howls and catcalls.

Meanwhile, Althea's opponent comes running from the opposite side of the court. Angela envelops Althea in a giant hug, protecting her from view, and then walks her toward the dressing room. When the judges want to disqualify Althea from the competition because of this apparent code violation, Angela won't allow it. Althea is not only her opponent, but her friend—both on and off the court.

A lot of the common ground that formed the foundation of Angela and Althea's friendship was tennis. They competed against each other, they played doubles together, and they even won both the Wimbledon Championships and French Open together as doubles partners in 1956. They traveled together to tennis matches, and Althea considered Angela's mother's house her second home. But they were also both outsiders, rejected by the white tennis establishment of the 1950s. African American Althea and Jewish Angela were each excluded from elite tennis clubs because of racial and religious prejudice. They had obstacles to overcome, but instead of going it alone, Angela and Althea supported each other, forging a bond of friendship that lasted throughout their lives, even after they retired their rackets.

> **"No matter what accomplishments you make, somebody helped you."** *(Althea Gibson)*

ACTIVITY 3

Friendship isn't always smooth sailing. Of course there are times when friends don't get along. Recall a time when you and a friend had a fight or disagreement. Fill in the concept map below with a description of the problem that caused the rift, the way you solved the problem, and how you resolved the issue in your friendship.

PROBLEM

SOLUTION

RESOLUTION

WHAT I THINK

Next to family, friends are probably the most important people in the world to us. Enduring friendships involve sharing and compromise, and can only be built on a foundation of giving.

1. Write a friendship manual, with step-by-step instructions about how to be a friend. The manual may contain sections including "Before You Begin," "Troubleshooting," and "Frequently Asked Questions."

2. Make a list of people who have done something kind for you. Include at least two friends and describe what they did for you.

3. Make a list of kind things you have done for your friends in the last week.

4. Our tradition instructs us to say a certain blessing of thanksgiving when we see a friend whom we haven't seen for more than thirty days. But why wait thirty days? Seek out an opportunity to thank God for your friendships right now by expressing your thanks out loud and in your own words.

5. Write a letter of apology to a friend for something you may have done that hurt his or her feelings. Is it easier to ask forgiveness or to forgive someone else? Why?

CHAPTER 3

Koach Hadibur

As soon as the words left his mouth, the boy regretted having thought them, let alone spoken them. He asked his rabbi how to make amends.

"Buy a bag of seeds, then scatter the seeds into the wind," the rabbi advised.

The boy did as he was told, returning to the rabbi to report on his success. "I scattered the seeds, Rabbi. Now what?"

"Now go back to the same spot and pick up all the seeds you scattered."

"Pick them all up?" the boy protested. "That's impossible. By now those seeds have been blown all over the place by the wind or picked up by birds. They may have even taken root in the dirt."

"Exactly my point," said the rabbi. "Your words are like seeds. It's impossible to retrieve them once they leave your mouth. Next time, make sure the words you speak are words you don't need to retrieve."

(Jewish folktale)

The Power of Speech

When God created the world, God gave us a powerful and awesome gift that makes us unique among the creations: כֹּחַ הַדִּבּוּר *(koach hadibur)*, the power of speech. By using this power as it was intended, we have the ability to build relationships with others and with God. We can communicate our hopes and fears; we can share our thoughts and ideas; we can encourage, motivate, and inspire. If, however, we abuse the power of speech, we risk destroying the very foundations upon which relationships are built. Gossip, rumors, lies, and hurtful or disrespectful words all undermine relationships. Therefore, Jewish tradition teaches us how to use our speech for positive, constructive purposes (offering a compliment or word of encouragement) and offers guidance on how to avoid destructive communication (rude remarks, slander, or harmful words).

FREEDOM OF SPEECH

One of the freedoms we enjoy in the United States is our freedom of speech. We each have the legal right to voice our opinions publicly. But, not surprisingly, freedom of speech has its limits. For example, certain kinds of hate speech are forbidden by American law. As Jews, we follow the Torah's guidelines for how people should speak to each other and how people should speak out on behalf of others. *L'shon hara* (true but derogatory talk about another person), *motzi shem ra* (untrue derogatory talk), and *r'chilut* (gossiping) are all considered misuse of the gift of speech.

ACTIVITY 1

Our sages compare speech to an arrow. Once our words are released, they can never be stopped. Even if we aim our words at a particular target, they can easily go astray. In today's fast-paced digital society, our words can travel faster and have greater impact than ever before.

Assume that Liz told something private to her friend James. If James told two people, who each told two people, how many people know Liz's secret? Use the diagram to the right to calculate your answer. _____

Now assume that James told three people, who each told three people. Draw a diagram to illustrate the path Liz's secret traveled.

How many people know Liz's secret now? _____

By James telling one additional person Liz's private information, how many additional people found out about it? _____

How many people would know Liz's secret if James hadn't told anyone? _____

How Do You Handle Negative Speech?

Take this quiz to find out.

When a group of friends gossips about a classmate, you:

◆ Try very hard to change the subject.

◆ Tell your friends nice things about the classmate.

◆ Tell your friends not to be so sneaky and so nosy.

When your best friend loses her temper, she curses, so you:

◆ Walk away until the tantrum ends.

◆ Remind her that because she's striving to become more holy, she shouldn't speak like that.

◆ Tell her that cursing is not cool and she should stop.

When your classmates make fun of another student, you tell them to stop because:

◆ The guy being teased wouldn't like it.

◆ The student is a good person and never did anything to hurt anyone.

◆ It is hurtful to call people mean names.

When you're accused of something that someone else did, you:

◆ Declare your innocence but refuse to say more.

◆ Reveal the guilty party but try to remain nonjudgmental.

◆ Privately urge the guilty party to confess.

When your friends start to fight with each other, you:

◆ Leave the room before they involve you in their argument.

◆ Tell one friend that the other was just trying to make him laugh.

◆ Suggest that they take time out to think about what they said.

Mostly red
Stay out of it
You're smart enough to walk away from gossip because you know that it "kills three people: the speaker, the listener, and the person being discussed" *(Talmud, Arachin 15b).*

Mostly green
Stay positive
Unlike those who can only tear down people with damaging words, you are able to repair hurt feelings with gentle yet powerful speech, as it says, "Pleasant words are like a honeycomb, sweet to the palate and a cure for the body" *(Proverbs 16:24).*

Mostly blue
Stay true to your values
You are fearless when confronting people—including friends—who abuse their power of speech, and you often encourage them to change their ways, as it says, "A love without rebuke is no love" *(Genesis Rabbah 54:3).*

AGADDIC TRADITION

Two rabbis had lunch together at a kosher restaurant somewhere in Poland. When they finished their meal, the owner asked how they liked the food.

"It was delicious," replied Rabbi Israel Meir Kagan, better known as the Chofetz Chaim.

"It was good," added the other rabbi, "but the soup was a little salty."

"I can't believe what you just said!" exclaimed the Chofetz Chaim to his companion when the woman returned to the kitchen. "How could you talk like that?"

The other rabbi was taken aback. "What did I do? I said the food was good. I added that it was a little on the salty side, but that's the truth."

"You don't get it," answered the Chofetz Chaim. "The owner probably doesn't prepare the food here. She has a cook who may need this job to support her family. Because of what you said, the owner will yell at the cook for preparing salty food. The cook will say that the food isn't salty. They will argue, calling each other names, and in the end, the cook will be fired. Then what will be with her family? Your comment will cause an argument and lose the cook—who is a fine cook—her job."

"Don't you think you're blowing this out of proportion?" came the other's response. "A comment about food—especially when I said the food was good—can't possibly have so much power."

"That's what you think. Follow me to the kitchen and see for yourself the power of your words."

The two rabbis indeed found the restaurant owner and cook in mid-argument.

"Forgive me," interrupted the Chofetz Chaim's companion. "I am so sorry for causing trouble. The food really was good. Everyone has different tastes when it comes to food and salt. Please don't be hard on the cook."

As they left the restaurant that afternoon, the Chofetz Chaim commented to his companion, "Imagine if you had complimented the cook on the soup. Imagine if you had said it was the best soup you've had all week. Your words have the power to build or to destroy."

ACTIVITY 2

How does it feel when someone compliments or criticizes your work? _____

How can expressing an honest opinion hurt another person? _____

Do you think the Chofetz Chaim overreacted? Explain your answer. _____
_____

KOACH HADIBUR SUPERSTAR: DEBORAH TANNEN

The table was set, the guests had arrived, and the turkey was ready to be carved. But Steve, the host, was annoyed by the unusual centerpiece—Deborah Tannen's tape recorder. It was Thanksgiving and Steve had graciously invited five friends to his home in Berkeley, California, for the holiday dinner. But Deborah Tannen, a friend and doctoral candidate in linguistics, had brought along her tape recorder. She was studying conversations and hoped that the Thanksgiving dinner conversation of six friends from across the globe would prove interesting for her research.

And it did. In fact, it formed the foundation of a career of research, writing, and teaching about conversational styles. When Deborah analyzed the Thanksgiving dinner tapes, she paid close attention to how each speaker paced what they had to say, charted the number of words spoken on each topic, and timed each speaker's pauses. She puzzled over why some people spoke more often and at greater length than others.

Deborah's analysis of the Thanksgiving dinner in Berkeley pinpointed two main conversational styles, what she calls "high-involvement" speakers and "high-considerateness" speakers. High-involvement speakers show their interest in others by talking along and leaving brief, if any, pauses to keep the conversation going. High-considerateness speakers, on the other hand, show concern for others by not imposing and leaving longer pauses. The speakers waiting for longer pauses end up getting interrupted by the speakers who are just trying to be enthusiastic listeners. By understanding the differences in our friends' speech styles, we can often clear up misunderstandings or avoid taking—or giving—offense.

In addition to studying conversations between friends, sociolinguist Deborah Tannen also studies the impact of conversational style on relationships between men and women, sibling relationships, and arguments.

> "We all want, above all, to be heard—but not merely to be heard. We want to be understood—heard for what we think we are saying, for what we know we meant."

Koach Hadibur

People gossip for a variety of reasons. They may do it to feel superior to others, for attention, or out of anger or unhappiness. A juicy piece of gossip can sometimes be hard to resist, but we know that it can be hurtful and cruel. Here are four tactics you can use to avoid getting mixed up in gossiping conversations.

Tactic: *Interrupt and change the subject.*

What can you say to change the subject?

_____

_____

How is changing the subject an effective response to gossip? _____

_____

_____

Tactic: *Walk away from the group of gossipers.*

How is walking away an effective response to gossip?

_____

_____

_____

Where might you go so that you don't feel alone or left out? _____

_____

_____

Photo Gallery

Tactic: *Stand up for the target.*

What can you say to show the gossipers that you side with their target? _____
_____
_____

How is standing up for the target an effective response to gossip? _____
_____
_____

Tactic: *Rebuke the gossiper.*

How can you rebuke a friend in a way that he or she will actually listen? _____
_____
_____
_____

How is rebuke an effective response to gossip? _____
_____
_____

ACTIVITY 3

Start a "Power Hour." Decide to use your power of speech wisely during a set hour each day for two weeks. During this time, be conscious of your words and concentrate on avoiding hurtful, angry, or mean speech. Write down your chosen hour on the clocks below. Use the calendar to check off your successes.

am pm *until* **am pm**

SUNDAY	MONDAY	TUESDAY	WEDNESDAY	THURSDAY	FRIDAY	SHABBAT
SUNDAY	MONDAY	TUESDAY	WEDNESDAY	THURSDAY	FRIDAY	SHABBAT

Tips:

1. Choose an hour that is relatively easy for you, not a time when you know you will be tempted to gossip.

2. Make sure that you don't forget when your Power Hour starts. Try setting an alarm on your cell phone or ask a friend or family member to remind you.

3. Avoid talking about specific people. Focus your conversation, instead, on what you've learned in school or some other neutral topic.

4. Change the topic if a friend starts to speak in a negative way. Prepare a topic or two in advance so you won't have to think on your feet.

WHAT I THINK

"Not everything that is thought should be expressed, not everything that is expressed should be written, and not everything that is written should be published." *(Rabbi Israel Salanter)*

1. What is the benefit of expressing your thoughts? What might be a drawback to expressing every thought?

2. How does Rabbi Salanter's statement relate to texting, social media, small talk, and other informal conversation?

3. Why do you think people use derogatory names and racial slurs? How can you speak out against destructive language?

4. For one day, write down some of the things you say to other people. At the end of the day, look over your notes and ask yourself how your words may have affected others. Is there anything you wish you hadn't said?

CHAPTER 4

Ometz Lev

Queen Esther was acutely aware of the blood pumping through her veins and the sweat making her palms slippery and uncomfortable. She was embarking on a potentially suicidal rescue mission, inspired by Mordechai's moving words: "If you remain silent at a time like this, relief and deliverance will come to the Jews from another place, while you will perish. And who knows whether it was just for such a time as this that you attained royalty."

Trusting in God and in the righteousness of her cause, Esther did what she knew she must do. She said a quick prayer and then took a step forward into the king's inner chamber. Ahashverosh noticed her right away. He was both surprised and curious to see her standing there—surprised that she would dare approach him without being summoned and curious what could be so important to her that she would risk her life for it. His curiosity winning out, King Ahashverosh extended his scepter to his queen, setting in motion a series of events that would save the Jewish people from certain annihilation. *(Megillat Esther)*

Courage

The dictionary may define courage as fearlessness, but Jewish tradition doesn't. אֹמֶץ לֵב *(ometz lev)* means choosing to do what is right over what is easy. Any time we stand up for what we believe in, resist negative peer pressure, or exercise self-control, we are demonstrating *ometz lev,* which literally means "strength of heart." We may be scared stiff as we confront a bully or stand up for our convictions, but if we do what's right despite the fear, then we are courageous.

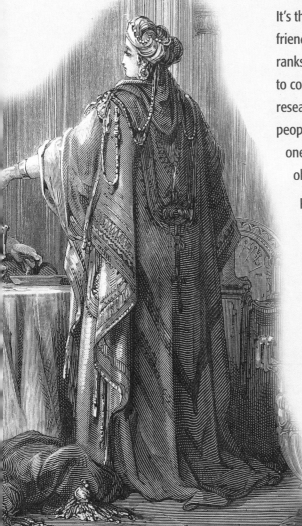

PEER PRESSURE

It's the latest craze and all your friends are doing it. Or maybe your friends aren't doing it, but the "in" crowd is, and you'd like to join their ranks. Should you do it too? Psychologists tell us that the temptation to conform is very strong. A landmark study by researcher Solomon Asch found that on average people will agree with what the majority says one-third of the time, even when the majority is obviously wrong.

Resisting the pressure to conform can be really hard sometimes and requires real courage. The good news is that this courage is already inside of you. According to the Ramban, a thirteenth-century Jewish scholar and leader, God does not test a person unless that person can overcome the test. This means that each of us already has the tools—including a powerful arsenal of courage—to overcome the challenges we face. We just have to learn to tap into our spiritual reserves when we are tested with peer pressure and other stressful challenges.

ACTIVITY 1

In order to stand up for your beliefs and convictions, it's important to clarify what's important to you. On a scale of 1 to 5, circle the number indicating how you feel about each statement below. When you are finished, put a star next to each statement that you feel is so important that it's worth taking a stand when others disagree.

	STRONGLY DISAGREE		NEUTRAL		STRONGLY AGREE
People must report cheating when they see it.	1	2	3	4	5
Kids should never make fun of other people.	1	2	3	4	5
Parents must approve of all of their child's friends.	1	2	3	4	5
Every Jewish child should go to religious school.	1	2	3	4	5
It's important to support Israel with our words and actions at all times.	1	2	3	4	5
All Jews should keep kosher.	1	2	3	4	5
Kids should be allowed to own cell phones.	1	2	3	4	5
It's okay to borrow something without permission.	1	2	3	4	5
It's important to look nice and fashionable.	1	2	3	4	5
People should always tell the truth.	1	2	3	4	5
Friends should help protect each other from bullies.	1	2	3	4	5
People should never do drugs.	1	2	3	4	5
All Jewish institutions should be handicap accessible.	1	2	3	4	5
It's important to treat sports opponents with respect.	1	2	3	4	5

List one more belief about which you feel strongly. _____
_____

Are You a Creature of Courage?

Take this quiz and find out.

Your friends invite you to skip school with them. When you decline, they call you a goody-goody. You:

◆ Walk away and go find other friends to hang out with.

◆ Tell them to have a good time and that you'll catch up with them tomorrow in school.

◆ Tell them they're wasting their time if they think put-downs can make you change your mind.

The kid who bullied your little brother last year is running for class president. You:

◆ Join his opponent's campaign.

◆ Don't vote for him and figure that if he wins, he must be qualified despite his negative past.

◆ Show up at a debate and ask the candidates to pledge that they will treat others respectfully.

A disabled boy in your class wants to join you and your friends at your favorite hangout, but there's no ramp for his wheelchair. You never noticed before, but now you:

◆ Make plans with friends to hang out somewhere else so he can come along.

◆ Write a letter requesting that the owners build a ramp and then hope for the best.

◆ March right over there and complain to the manager.

A family across town lost everything in a fire. When you hear about it, you:

◆ Donate your allowance to the synagogue drive on their behalf.

◆ Pull together some soft blankets, books, and snacks, then take them to the house where they are staying temporarily.

◆ Ask people to donate household goods and organize a drop-off location at your school.

Mostly red
Galloping Gazelle

You welcome the support of others who share your values. Like the gazelle who travels in a great herd, you find strength in numbers. You know well the teaching of the following midrash: "When a person takes a bunch of reeds, it is hard to tear apart, but if reeds are taken alone, even a child can break them" *(Tanchuma Nitzavim 1).*

Mostly green
Lone Wolf

What matters most to you is doing what's right and acting according to your values. You don't try to convince others to share your opinion, but prefer to follow the advice of the Talmud: "First correct yourself and only then correct others" *(Bava Batra 60b).*

Mostly blue
Roaring Lion

You always stand up for what you know is right, even if it means confronting authority. You're eager to take charge and change things for the best, and you'll work hard to make others see what you know to be true. The words of Psalm 27:3 speak to you: "Should an army besiege me, my heart would have no fear; should a war arise against me, still I would be confident."

AGADDIC TRADITION

David sat in the shade of a carob tree beside his friend Jonathan. The tree's overhanging branches provided sufficient cover to keep their conversation private.

"Do you think anyone will see us, David?" Jonathan asked anxiously. "If word gets back to my father, King Saul, you'll be a goner. Yesterday, Father told all his servants again about his plans to kill you."

"Kill me? Again?" David cried, jumping to his feet. This wouldn't be King Saul's first attempt to assassinate David. "Why does King Saul hate me so? What have I done? I put my life in my hands when I slew the giant Goliath, and God granted a great salvation to all of Israel. King Saul saw it and rejoiced. He appointed me over the warriors. So why does he now seek my life?"

"He's jealous, David," Jonathan replied, motioning for David to sit. "As crazy as it sounds, he sees you as a threat to the security of his royal throne. He knows that God is with you, and it frightens him."

"You're his son and you're my best friend. Tell him that I have no desire for the throne," David pleaded.

"David, I've already tried countless times. Listen to me," Jonathan began, rising to his feet. A speech like this couldn't be made sitting down. Jonathan met David's eyes as he spoke slowly and carefully. "I love you, my friend, as I love myself. We sealed a covenant of friendship years ago because we recognized that our souls are attached. I've never had a friend like you before, David, and I won't let you die at my father's hand. Hear me, David, you shall not die!"

True to his word, Jonathan repeatedly saved David's life by intervening with King Saul, sending David into hiding, and helping David escape to safety.

ACTIVITY 2

In addition to dealing with Saul's assassination attempts, David had to cope with many other challenging situations in his life. His psalms can serve as inspiration, and repeating them to ourselves in our own challenging times will help build courage. Here are some examples.

"Be strong and let your hearts take courage, all you who hope in God." *(Psalm 31:25)*

"This poor man calls and God hears, and from all his troubles God saves him." *(Psalm 34:7)*

"Cast upon God your burden and God will sustain you." *(Psalm 55:23)*

"In God I have trusted, I shall not fear." *(Psalm 56:12)*

How can faith in God help believers build strength of heart and courage? _____

_____

_____

OMETZ LEV SUPERSTAR: ALAN SUSSMAN

Alan and Sheldon had been friends for almost thirty years. Together they led a Jewish learning group, and their families were close. When Alan learned that Sheldon was ill and needed a transplant, he was shocked. He heard that Sheldon needed a kidney from a donor with A+ blood. Although his blood type is also A+, Alan's initial reaction to the coincidence was fear and rejection.

As the news sank in, determination replaced Alan's fear. All of Sheldon's family members had been rejected as potential kidney donors, and the waiting list for cadaver kidneys was way too long. The more he thought about it, the more Alan realized that donating his kidney to his close friend made sense.

The operation was not simple, but it was indeed successful in saving Sheldon's life. In fact, Alan's kidney began to function in Sheldon's body immediately.

When Alan awoke the day after surgery in his hospital bed, he was in pain, yet he felt absolutely wonderful. "I could not yet sit up in bed," he recalls, "but I felt strong." Over the next few days, the hospital staff kept track of Alan's milestones: sitting up, standing, eating solid food, and learning to go to the bathroom. But the highlight, says Alan, was his first walk to the other side of the ward to visit his friend Sheldon. "There were hugs all around and picture taking," he remembers.

> "I have been through so many tests and had so much blood drawn that it is a wonder I have any left. But with each test and procedure, I learned about an inner strength I never knew I had. I felt stronger and more confident each time. For once in my life I had the power to stand toe-to-toe with the Angel of Death, look him in the eye and say, 'No, not this time, not this one. You can't have him.'"

Ometz Lev

Here are strategies that can make it easier to step out of your comfort zone and act courageously:

1. *Give yourself a pep talk. Remind yourself that others have done it, that it won't be as hard as you think, or choose another motivating mantra.*
2. *Practice courage. If you're facing something big, practice your courage on something smaller to boost your confidence. For example, rehearse what you'll say at a confrontation or try asserting yourself on easier issues.*
3. *Seek guidance. A friend or adult may be able to help. There's no reason to go it alone.*

Try out these strategies in each of the following challenging situations.

Challenge: *Befriending the new kid, who is different*

1. My pep talk: "_____
_____"

2. How I can practice: _____
_____

3. I can seek guidance from: _____
_____

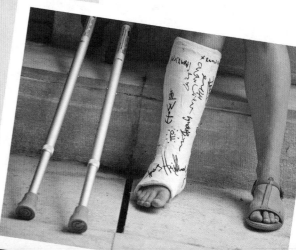

Challenge: *Dealing with injury and pain*

1. My pep talk: "_____
_____
_____"

2. How I can practice: _____
_____
_____

3. I can seek guidance from: _____
_____
_____

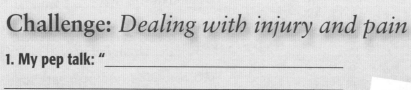

Photo Gallery

Challenge: *Saying no to a friend's offer of a cigarette*

1. My pep talk: "_____
_____
_____ "

2. How I can practice: _____
_____
_____

3. I can seek guidance from: _____
_____
_____

Challenge: *Defending a friend against bullying*

1. My pep talk: "_____
_____ "

2. How I can practice: _____
_____

3. I can seek guidance from: _____
_____

ACTIVITY 3

Overcoming challenges builds our courage muscles. For each category listed below, consider a time in your life that you had to display courage in the face of a difficult situation. Describe the experience briefly in the center of each barbell. Then write down the risks or challenges you confronted at the time and what the benefits were to you.

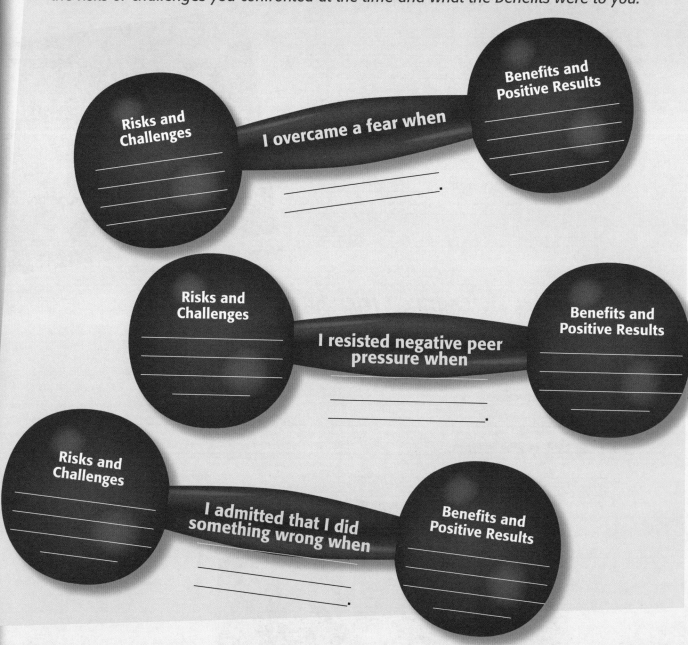

Risks and Challenges

Benefits and Positive Results

I overcame a fear when

Risks and Challenges

Benefits and Positive Results

I resisted negative peer pressure when

Risks and Challenges

Benefits and Positive Results

I admitted that I did something wrong when

WHAT I THINK

"Courage is a special kind of knowledge: the knowledge of how to fear what ought to be feared and how not to fear what ought not to be feared." *(David Ben-Gurion)*

1. Make a list of fears that you think are normal.

2. Make another list of things you think people are afraid of but shouldn't be.

3. It takes courage to voice your opinion. Choose a cause in today's world about which you feel strongly and that you think needs change. Design a poster that you can use to publicize this issue. How else can you make your voice heard?

4. Design a medal of honor or achievement award for a courageous person you know. You can draft the language and sketch a logo for the award, then personalize it for the honoree you have in mind.

CONCLUSION

In **Be a Good Friend**, which is the third volume in the *Living Jewish Values* series, we have explored these four Jewish values that help build meaningful friendships:

Dan L'chaf Zechut—Judging Favorably

Reyut—Friendship

Koach Hadibur—The Power of Speech

Ometz Lev—Courage

In volume 2, *Family Connections*, we investigated four values that strengthen family relations:

Hakarat Hatov—Gratitude

Sh'lom Bayit—Family Harmony

Emet—Truth

Kedushah—Holiness

In volume 1, *Be Your Best Self*, we studied four values that foster personal growth:

K'vod Habriyot—Individual Dignity

T'shuvah—Returning to Your Best Self

Sameach B'chelko—Personal Satisfaction

Anavah—Humility

All together, we have discussed twelve Jewish values in the *Living Jewish Values* series. Adopting these values as part of your life takes practice but will help you grow into an even better person and the best possible friend.

For each of the values in the diagram to the right, fill in the space with one thing you remember about the value. It may be a definition of the value, a core text associated with it, a relevant story, or a strategy you will use to adopt the value. Since this is a book about friendship, we encourage you to complete this exercise with a friend!

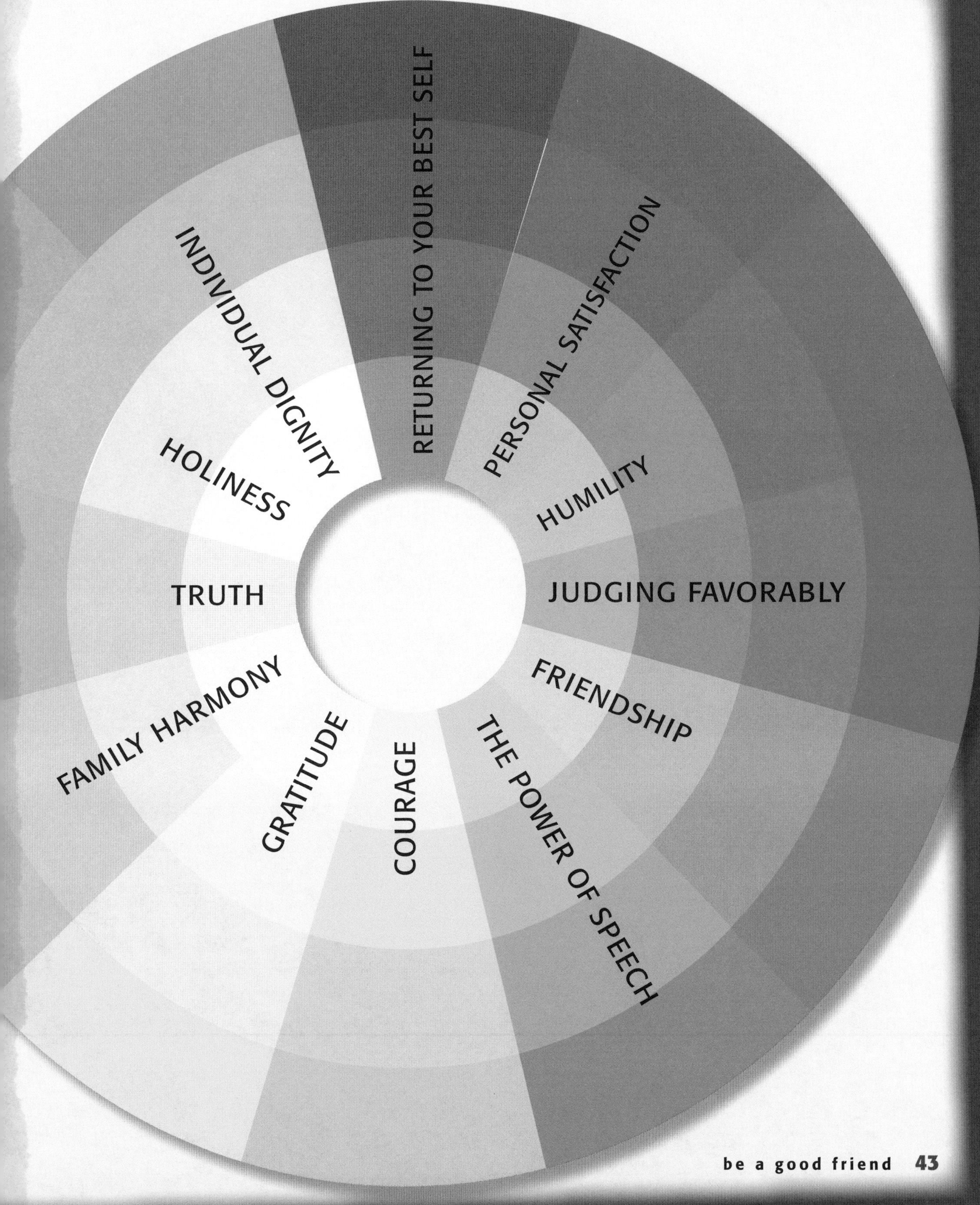

INDIVIDUAL DIGNITY

RETURNING TO YOUR BEST SELF

PERSONAL SATISFACTION

HOLINESS

HUMILITY

TRUTH

JUDGING FAVORABLY

FAMILY HARMONY

FRIENDSHIP

GRATITUDE

COURAGE

THE POWER OF SPEECH